What Word When

by

William Hulstine

Bloomington, IN  Milton Keynes, UK

AuthorHouse™
1663 Liberty Drive, Suite 200
Bloomington, IN 47403
www.authorhouse.com
Phone: 1-800-839-8640

AuthorHouse™ UK Ltd.
500 Avebury Boulevard
Central Milton Keynes, MK9 2BE
www.authorhouse.co.uk
Phone: 08001974150

First published by AuthorHouse 8/29/2006

Library of Congress Control Number: 2005903994

ISBN: 1-4208-5183-7 (sc)

Printed in the United States of America
Bloomington, Indiana

This book is printed on acid-free paper.

APPRECIATION

IT WOULDN'T BE FAIR TO PRODUCE A BOOK SUCH AS THIS WITHOUT EXPRESSING MY GRATITUDE TO THE LATE MRS HEBINKS, AN EIGHTH-GRADE ENGLISH TEACHER IN WEST VIRGINIA TEACHING AT MORGANTOWN JUNIOR HIGH SCHOOL. SHE HAD A MARVELOUS WAY OF AROUSING MY INTEREST IN ENGLISH GRAMMAR AND LITERATURE. WITHOUT THE BACKGROUND RECEIVED FROM HER TEACHING CAPABILITIES, THIS BOOK WOULD NOT HAVE BEEN WRITTEN.

I ALSO WISH TO EXPRESS MY THANKS TO MY WIFE SHERRY AND DAUGHTER JULIE FOR THE TIME EACH OF THEM DEDICATED TO CRITIQUING THE MANUSCRIPT.

PREFACE

This collection was produced solely for young students, to enhance their knowledge of the complicated English language. **The words underlined have the same pronunciation but different spellings and different descriptions.**

The purpose of this book is to provide students with information that will help them learn new English words and be original and creative in using them to design their personal sentences, paragraphs, essays, stories, reports, etc. using underlined words and sentences as examples. Once given the assignment, they would be inspired to research unknown and unfamiliar words in the dictionary and create literature, whether it would be humorous, eerie, romantic, weird, rhyming, fiction, truth, an experience, or any combination. Educational improvement in the use of words would be exceptional. **The challenge would be to be creative using their individual ingenuity and research in their originations**.

It is believed students would actually enjoy their own work while they would be learning the meanings and usage of unfamiliar words.

This book is intended for grade levels beginning with the second or third grade and advancing upward. It would be the teacher's/instructor's responsibility to determine which words would be appropriate for which education level.

This author did not peruse the "new words section" of the dictionary, nor the areas with groups of prefixes such as in-, non-, over-, pre-, re-, un-, or well-. There are several hundred of these, and it would have been repetitious to mate them up with additional sentences.

All underlined words were found in *Webster's Encyclopedic Unabridged Dictionary,* but other large unabridged dictionaries such as *The American Heritage Dictionary of the English Language* will also include the underlined words. If such dictionaries are unavailable in the school, the student would have to visit a public library for research.

A

A skater tried to perform an axel while carrying an axle, but fell on his posterior.

We will all benefit if we learn to use the awl adeptly.

Austin will alter the altar before the morning service commences.

Let's aid the aide with a glass of water.

Chad, let's add more descriptive words to the ad.

Dale, you will ail if you consume too much ale.

He has been weird and acts like an axe fell on his head.

A famous sailor hit his eye with his pipe and replied, "Aye, sir, I have a sore eye."

Aw, most people are in awe of deity.

Anna was collecting some fascinating ana.

The augur was almost ready to use an auger.

Noah was concerned because his ark had a huge arc near the bow.

Perhaps residents on Argo would communicate in argot.

He was not allowed to utter anything aloud.

Let's ante, then Auntie Eleanor
can deal the cards.

Apparently Abel was not able to
defend himself against Cain.

Aunt Lola was bitten by a giant ant.

Search these out and impress your
instructor — acclamation and acclimation.

In biochemistry there is actin and
centuries ago there was acton.

It would be nice to say adieu to ado!

The eagle was constructing an airy aery aerie.

His lawyer is going to airship a copy of
the will and the heirship of the heir.

In the field of biochemistry, one could
find albumin but not albumen.

Amygdalin is related to chemicals,
but amygdaline is related to nuts.

Make an appointment to send
the annalist to an analyst.

An anchorite would not want to
experiment with ankerite.

Anger and angor could be closely related.

The nouns apophasis and apophysis are
unrelated. Research and originate your ideas.

In math, one may hear the word
apothem, but not the word apothegm.

Aril in botany is not related
to aryl in chemistry.

She gave her assent for the
ascent to the top floor.

Our captain said, "Anchors aweigh
mates, so we can sail away."

It would be awful if we had to eat some offal.

B

At the entrance, Nell the lovely
belle will ring the bell.

The bass singers will occupy
the base row of the choir.

He cannot bore a hole adequate
for a boar to enter.

When the captain landed on shore, the bow
of his boat tore a bough from a tree.

Aunt Bea thought we should be busy
as a bee. Isn't English fun?

Buck did not know whether to
squeeze the beet or beat it.

If we get a bye for our game, we will
have time to buy some baseballs
at the store by our house.

This is a nice rifle, but the butt is damaged.

The word bate has several different
meanings and is not related to bait.

Son, don't bawl because you lost the ball.

The bear will have bare essentials
where he is taken for care.

The cotton pickers placed the boll
in that bowl by the bole.

My beau launched an arrow from his bow.

The bale of goods is sinking our boat, so let's bail fast.

Banc referring to law and judges is not akin to a bank.

The baron was very troubled when he discovered he was barren.

Becky arrived at the beach but did not see any beech trees.

Barry was cautious not to bury the berry patch while dumping dirt.

We have been anxious to commence loading the bin.

He will birl the log with a burl on it.

Brr, it's cold, and the man with the birr may cut his hand with the bur or the burr.

Use the ¾ bit to produce four holes in the bitt of the vessel.

The school bloc will meet to determine which type of block to utilize.

We all became bored with the decision of the board.

Bogey, bogie, and bogy are interesting — look them up for different descriptions.

Boots is the only dog we are aware of that was born on a borne.

The boy was surprised when he discovered that buoy has two different pronunciations.

A computer byte is totally unrelated to an ant bite.

We must train our burro to burrow holes, and eliminate the moles.

If the breech of his body hits the floor, would that constitute a breach of contract?

The two rats that were bred in the lab would not eat bread.

We need some burly men to pick the burley.

She was chasing a large bat that flew into the batt on our clothesline.

The bard was arrested for forgery and barred from future publications forever.

Many years ago, the birth of a berth came about.

Let's blend the blende to produce something interesting.

After the destruction of his boat, we expected some bote.

The bach was producing a batch of cookies.

Baylee was in the bailey when she became a bailee.

Three bands will be hired for the banns announcements.

A female officer named Billie has
a fourteen-pound billy.

Blanche insisted it was time
to blanch the material.

On the brim of the canyon we opted to
descend to the lake to catch bream.

Bill will be careful not to break the
new brake while installing it.

We brewed up some tea for the
brood of kinfolk coming.

We concocted some special brews in
hopes they would soothe his bruise.

Unfortunately, the groom could not
sweep away the brume with a broom.

The brute had too much brut wine and
was about to bruit at a group of people.

While on the bus, he was hoping to
receive a buss from his female friend.

At sea, we adjusted the bibb then put
on the baby's bib so she could eat.

C

Perhaps Cain slew Abel with a cane.

Cary lost a valuable coin while constructing the quoin.

Cristie will play chords properly by strumming the correct cords.

The sound of the cymbal will be the symbol.

He has a cache of cash in the safe at his house.

At the pet store, the birds that don't cheep are the cheap ones.

Chelsi will cede the seed to her little brother.

The core of our troops abroad is the Marine Corps.

It would be weird to see a canon firing the cannon.

If you climb the creek to the peak, your bones will creak.

On the computer, click the correct buttons to join the right clique.

The officer will cite him on sight if he returns to the site after the fight.

We can canvass the neighborhood to locate some canvas.

Have we enough capital to travel to Washington, DC to view our Capitol?

Some world-famous rabbits would appreciate a definition of carrot, carat, and karat.

We do not want to cast insults on that caste of highly educated people.

The cellar is where the seller will be displaying his wares.

In our cartoon filming we decided to use a cel, but could not sell the idea of a cell.

The cession occurred after a fourteen-hour session between David and Goliath.

Cambrie thought it possible cetin could be used in the manufacture of seton.

This is the right course, though the mountain has a very coarse terrain.

The cubicle office where she is employed is actually cubical.

Let's put together a crew capable of arranging a very special krewe.

We bought a came for our window, and discovered a kame due to the cold weather.

In the office of the censor, a censer caused the sensor to respond.

In the cask was a small casque.

At the circus we might find a cercus
if we had a microscope.

We spent many hours looking for cereus
then decided to get serious about it.

That callous individual deserved
the callus he got.

Let's put up the canopy then
partake of some canapé.

The cantor was riding his horse
at a continuous canter.

Let's have a bowl of hot chili so
we don't get chilly, silly.

His face and collar both turned
red because of his choler.

England and France were in concord
when they built the Concorde.

Please put on a coat then go
out and check the cote.

The council decided to give counsel to
those deemed necessary to receive it.

The counselor found it necessary to
advise the councilor of his duties.

We decided to drive the coupe
to the chicken coop.

If we had a crock large enough
we could cook a croc.

Crows would not trip over the croze in a barrel.

A famous sailor could not find a cruse while out on his cruise.

Our current currant patch is very healthy.

Our daughter Cicely went to Sicily but could not find any cicely.

Let's cart the kart out to the desert.

The colonel discovered a kernel in his pocket.

It required a lot of craft to build this widget, so wrap it carefully with kraft.

If we go riding, we must be prepared to caulk the calk if it comes off.

D

My dear, we must arise if we are going deer hunting.

Darren decided to desert the dessert while dieting.

Dew is due soon, so let's do chores now.

Derrick noticed the drupe on the tree was beginning to droop.

A doe smelled our pizza dough through our kitchen window.

Deanne, if the door is left open, a dor could enter, and perhaps many more.

If we daze Dad with a tap on the head, he may be able to remember the good old days.

Let's proceed to the restaurant and dine before we calculate the dyne.

Please do not damn the dam before they complete the construction of it.

Disc and disk are interesting, so investigate them for their meanings.

Let's meet out on the dock and don't forget to bring the doc.

Dustin is hoping he will not die of old age before the opportunity arises to dye eggs.

Check out the difference between debutant and debutante.

In Scotland, you may need to discern the difference between decern and discern.

In math, there is a del but it is not akin to a dell.

Would you believe dime and disme are pronounced the same?

The C.E.O. will dissent with the presentation, and cause the descent from his position.

After all negotiations, the warriors opted to have a dual duel.

In the biological world, one might deem a deme very intriguing.

His vehicle had so many dings, we called them dense dents.

The mason required dental work after being struck with a dentil.

The doctor will dole out instructions for the nurses and ask if there is a dol available.

Please don't dun him about something already done.

While dyeing Easter eggs, he discovered one of the eggs was dying.

The odd man we spoke of is a very discreet and discrete man.

The minister was donated a dossal and a dossil, but didn't have a clue what they were.

A dolman was discovered on the dolmen and it totally befuddled the professor.

E

At eight o'clock last night she
ate dinner on the ait.

She could earn money to purchase an
urn to inter her deceased erne.

Ere you take off in the air, remember
you are your father's only heir.

Erin was not eager to go near the beach
when she heard about the eagre coming.

Adam built Eve a house with only one eave.

Something is eerie about the
aerie and Lake Erie today.

The city council wanted to build an
el over the ell of our school.

Our elation had no false illation whatsoever.

We did not want to elicit an illicit
document for the court.

If we emerge from the raging water, we
don't want to immerge back into it.

Emersed and immersed could be opposites.

The entrants arrived at the
entrancc to the school.

When Ethel discovered the word
ethyl, she became bewildered.

The mountain is about to erupt so would that be a good time to irrupt the robber's house?

Eddie wants to go fishing in the eddy.

F

This weather today is foul, but the fowl are not concerned.

Is it fair to pay a fare to get to the fair? Isn't English entertaining?

Our dog Buddy was trying to flee from the fourteen-pound flea.

My flu was probably derived from that dirty flue, and the birds even flew away.

We constructed a fort which is our current forte.

We will perform a feat with our feet.

We think the floe will flow toward the beach, and wash up Davy Jones.

For dinner the friar would prefer a fryer.

Frank said we must be frank about this, because a franc is a coin in France.

For what reason are four golfers yelling fore?

It did not faze him as he endured the phase he was experiencing.

A person flying an aircraft could be called a flier, but a flyer is — look it up.

Before we freeze to death, let's modify the frieze so it is more attractive.

Let's go forth to the fourth cave and slay that dragon!

He fain would go to the fane, even if he had to feign good health.

Now here's a triple – fraise, frays, and phrase. Good luck researching!

Perhaps a fawn could be compared somewhat to a faun.

The word faint has different meanings, but feint has only one.

Several flocks of sheep are hanging out by the beautiful phlox.

Our foe turned out to be a faux enemy.

The flack was getting a lot of flak from his peers.

We lopped off limbs from our tree with a frow to keep it from swaying to and fro.

There is no flour in a flower.

There is a difference between fiancé and fiancée.

On our ranch, we have a filly that came from Philly.

If you take a flight to England you may want to investigate flite.

Let's review the facts before we fax them.

Did you fail to procure the faille?

Farci and farcy are interesting but not related.

That fellow has a cool felloe on his cycle.

You may have had a ferule used on you
but a ferrule could be a widget.

The Egyptians took a farrow
of pigs to the pharaoh.

We do not want to filter the philter
we give those lovebirds.

He was fined big bucks but we
could not find the reason why.

Wow, check out forehanded and
fourhanded and react responsibly!

A foreword is in the forward section of a book.

We had several frows but almost froze
while cutting the frozen meat.

G

Gene and Jean both have genes
and both like to wear jeans.

Gail almost became a victim of the gale.

The sun is shining on the glair, causing a glare.

The gnu will be new to the zoo,
and rhymes are fun too.

We groan more frequently after
we have grown older.

Our great-grandfather lost his mental
grip when he ailed with the grippe.

We guessed our guest was not
that famous vampire.

We noticed the groom had a grume on
his arm, so he went to the hospital.

The horse must slow his gait before entering
the gate, or become a headless horse.

Please gally the fat sailors if
they head for the galley.

My toothpaste is a gel, and
hopefully it will not jell.

Please do not gibe that famous
mermaid when she is trying to jibe.

It would not be prudent to manifest your
gloom because of the glume problem.

Wow, that is a great grate you purchased.

There really is a difference
between a grill and a grille.

Our horse is slow-gaited, but we still cannot
keep him in our gated community.

She did not want to gamble on
learning how to gambol.

When he attempted to gaff the
fish, he made a gaffe.

In medieval times, we may have
been able to gauge a gage.

That mare can gallop so well, we are
trying to train her to perform a galop.

The gopher became a gofer when
it was sent to dig a hole.

We had a natty maid who didn't care
for our gnatty house properly.

The gneiss we found is a nice one.

There will be no goby in the Gobi Desert.

The huge gourd was gored by a bull.

We sent our gorilla to capture
the bad guerrilla.

We need a greater grater for this task.

We could dye the greige gray.

Will we slip on grease if we enter Greece?

We decided to wear a gaiter on each leg when we went gator hunting.

He will grieve for his leg if the greave fails to function.

The grocer was not aware he was about to become grosser.

The guys had an awesome guise.

H

Hey, please put the hay in the barn.

A famous bunny is lamenting because he discovered a hare that had no hair.

Hi, let's hie to high ground to avoid the flood.

Let's assemble and hail our hale young hero.

After you halve it, we will have equal parts to share.

We heard your herd was doing well.

We can hire a famous web man to assist us in climbing higher up the mountain.

The doctor said he'll heal her heel in time for the deal.

Hurl the herl out to the fish, but do not catch that popular mermaid.

Sunday morning, the hymn will be sung by him or Jim.

Hey sweetie, if you provide a heer of linen, we will be here to hear you.

Please haul the books upstairs and deposit them in the hall.

Ho, guys, it's time to hoe weeds.

The horde of demonstrators stored a hoard of food for a future demonstration.

Let's not hew down the trees, because
they each have a different hue.

It would certainly be odd if our
horse became hoarse.

Let's reserve four hours that
will be ours together.

When our team makes the first hoop,
let's give them a real loud whoop.

He hurts because he knows
nothing about hertz.

The farmer was a little bit hicky
and even had a hickey.

He hied to hide in a safe place.
Isn't English amusing?

Get the four hoes and the hose,
and proceed to toil in the soil.

How's he going to house all those friends?

The handmaid was wearing a handmade apron.

Please hang the hanger in the hangar.

The hart has a large heart.

The heeler wanted to meet with the healer.

One might have a heaume in
his home on the holm.

The hecks on our looms were malfunctioning
as if someone had put a hex on them.

We knew our heroine was not using heroin.

In anatomy, one could say his shoulder had a humeral and humoral problem.

The problem with his humerus was not humorous.

The hippie was very hippy.

At the hostel, one might find some hostile teens.

The elderly, heirless man was found in an old, airless mansion.

I

I'll love you eternally if you remain on this isle until we marry and walk down the aisle.

Let's go in that awesome inn upon arrival.

The intern does not know what an inturn is.

We admire an idle idol who has plans to write an idyll.

She will indict you if you do not indite a document for the judge.

She had an eerie illusion that led to her elusion.

We must go back to the islet to find my lost eyelet.

Then we don't want to forget "I scream for ice cream." Ugh.

Because of his illusive nature, the seer became very elusive.

Idiograph and ideograph are unrelated but are both fascinating.

In anatomy, the ileum and ilium are both located in the same area of your body.

In anatomy, the adjectives ileac and iliac describe what?

That information is impartable and therefore impartible.

In Alaska, we reached an impassable area
but fortunately we were impassible people.

When in Indy, we tried
developing our own indie.

The teacher made an indiscreet review of his
essay and became indiscrete with his friends.

After we create our monster, let's give him
an insole for each foot, and ensoul him.

Install the insulant, whether
he is insolent or not.

She did not want to interrupt the
instillation of the installation.

Several instants passed before
the instance occurred.

We think the intention was
to raise the intension.

Let's gather and have an intercession
prior to intersession.

Interdental describes something in
your mouth, but what is interdentil?

Go research isotac and isotach
and write about them.

J

Julie will jest mildly as she relates the gest.

Janet, please don't jam the door jamb. Isn't English entertaining?

Jeannie has been desperately seeking a genie for fourteen years now.

We hoped the jinks being performed would not bring about a jinx on someone.

The prisoner found it difficult to jive with a gyve on his leg.

K

The koi are acting very coy today.

Let's proceed to the knap of the hill,
make camp, and enjoy a nap.

We know his answer will still be no.

Kohl is a cosmetic, but coal is a fuel.

Kola nuts provide cola.

He lives at the knob of the
hill on Nob Hill Road.

The key to the treasure is on
the cay off the mainland.

We knew her when she was new in our area.

The knight would fight ferociously for
his king in the light, or at night.

Kelcie began to knit and discovered
the nit of a louse in her house.

It would be nice to see a knave
in the nave of our church.

Knock on the door, the store owner
may open and show you a nock.

They may have keno in kino and
Reno. Rhyming is fun too.

L

Lucy forced the lamb on the lam.

I have lain in that lane before,
after a vehicle struck me.

Leora led us to the lead, but it
was too heavy to move.

He was on the lee side of the
mountain in the lea by the sea.

Let's issue a levy to place a tax on the levee.

Hey mate, please lock the gate into the loch.

Two awesome ducks discovered
a load of ore in the lode.

The lory is being transported by a lorry.

We made a loop around town to check
out a loupe at the jewelers.

Searching in the loot, she found an old lute.

Logan reeled that luce right up to
the boat, but it wiggled loose.

It's no lie that lye will burn your skin.

He could be a liar and a lier.

The leak in the hose will water
the leek efficiently.

It feels like our house is beginning to
lean because of the lien against it.

Please lay the lei in the lea. Isn't English super?

Mabel, if you're able, put the label on the table, but make sure it's not a labile table.

We cannot create shellac, because we lack the necessary lac.

The words lade and laid are both verbs and could be closely related.

Lew and Lou wanted to play some loo in lieu of Monopoly.

He must limn the limb by a sketch before we will understand its function.

Lo and behold, look how low it is over there.

After looting, one of the prizes broke and they needed some luting to repair it.

This hotel looks like it would provide very luxurious luxe.

If we lyse the lice, a metamorphosis may ensue, producing a group of Tyrannosaurs.

The lair of the bear resembled an oversize lehr.

We must not laze around today if we are going to lase our experiment.

The locks into the lochs are open, so let's catch salmon and make some lox.

Let's lessen the lesson for next week.

Larry acquired his loan from the
lone bank in Mayberry.

After many laps around the field,
the runner had a lapse.

They used a laser on the ape with lazar
and that famous giant gorilla emerged.

A leaf from his book blew away and
he pursued it as lief as he could.

If we leach the beach, we might find a leech.

Our invention lacks originality because
we were lax in our efforts.

The literal interpretation of the
word littoral is fascinating.

We loathe him because he is loath
to admit it when he errs.

The loon on the moon resembles
a lune. Rhyming is fun too.

Let us eat some lettuce — ugh.
English is outrageous isn't it?

M

Marilda thought the mail was being delivered by a male.

Yesterday morning, we were mourning the passing of our neighbor.

At Mary's ranch in Maine, her main horse has a large mane.

After fishing, let's meet to mete out the meat.

It seems like this mussel has muscle.

A mite might be dangerous to our health, if we eat it raw.

The miner will have only minor problems if he follows the rules.

It will require a millennium to inspect the mil of each wire in the mill.

Matt slipped on the mat, even though the floor had a matte finish.

We don't want the predator to maul someone in the mall.

Megan made the maid wash the dirty clothes.

The color of the maze was maize.

We all know what a mark is, but how about a marc and a marque?

In the morn, we must mourn for our dog.

We decided to muse regarding the mews emanating from Nakita.

A postal truck ran into a mailer and broke his malar bone.

The maser functioned properly until sparks rose from the mazer.

If we meddle in the right places, we might earn a medal.

If a marten possessed wings, perhaps it could catch a martin.

A manikin broke a store window and landed on a mannequin.

One would not find a Munsee in Muncie.

A certain animal must have a condition known as musth.

She mustered all her hunting ability and found some mustard.

What manner will we use when we speak to the owner of the manor?

Mike hung his mantle on the mantel and it became ashes.

That martial marshal was pursuing an infamous outlaw of the Old West.

It wouldn't be prudent to use marline to catch a marlin.

Ok, here's a duet to investigate
– mead, and meed.

Here's a triple to ponder – mean,
mesne, and mien. Isn't English fun?

Abraham Lincoln had great mettle,
but was not involved with metal.

The murre had an odor of myrrh.

In a moat, it would be difficult
to locate a mote.

Would you believe our mule
was beginning to mewl?

Before he mowed the lawn, he wanted to
find out what mode the motor was in.

It would not be appropriate for
a middy to wear a midi.

Here's a pair to research and report
about – miliary and milliary.

In the millinery world, it may be a
millenary time before men wear them.

You'll love these – moo, moue,
and last but foremost Mu.

It would be impossible to
mince up some mints.

The moose did not like our spicy mousse.

The miner mined until he lost his mind.

We all know what minks are,
but what about a minx?

Musicians would know about
mordent, but what is mordant?

A cruise missile is totally unrelated to a missal.

N

We were in the naval area, when
his navel began to itch.

Nina said there is a living
gnome in Nome, Alaska.

Her nose hurts and her doctor knows it.

Nan did not tie that knot.

We went to the buffet but there
was none left for the nun.

We need bread, so please knead the dough,
but don't get kneed in the process.

Uncle Nat was bitten by a
fourteen-pound gnat.

Nell was by the well when she heard the
knell of the bell. Rhyming is fun too.

Jack and his girlfriend went up the hill for
water and a nap, if they reach the nappe.

His wife was being naggy about the
knaggy sidewalk needing repair.

Many years ago we met some
nickers wearing knickers.

Nickie decided to nix the nicks and
proceed with the experiment.

Archery and nocks are not related to knocks.

The moose did not have a noose, but what about nous in Greek philosophy?

Luke was running from the nuke explosion and his nuque was injured.

O

If we desire the ore on that island we will need a paddle or an oar to get there.

Let's meet tomorrow at noon and we will have our hour together.

Everyone knows what odd means, but what about od?

Oh no, it appears I owe you fourteen dollars.

Please do not tramp on the awn planted on the lawn.

We will not oppose them if you agree to appose the items.

A cheetah may have ocellate spots and would be agile enough to oscillate.

He owed her compensation for the ode she created.

His company created an odeum but he had severe odium for it.

Hey, this is awesome — add some oleo to the olio.

He gave oral testimony regarding the aural manner of the defendant.

Our friend will overdo all the competition and the act is long overdue.

She oversees all the overseas deals.

Caution, be careful with overlade and overlaid.

He ought to know more than aught.

P

Please pare this pair of pears for the salad.

If we peer at the pier, the seer may appear. Rhyming is fun too.

The broken window pane will cause pain if it cuts you.

Paul was hit with a pail of water during the melee, and now he's pale.

We can use this pan to store the panne if we find some.

She heard by parol that she was up for parole.

It's par for fishing when we can't catch a parr.

We took Pa to see the pas at the ballet.

To keep peace, we gave him a piece of pie.

We must pique ourselves to reach the peak and have a peek if we're not too weak.

Let's listen to the peal of the bells while we peel fruit for our meal.

Computers have pica, but a pika might be found in the woods.

While in the flower bed, his pistol fired erroneously and shot off a pistil.

She leaned over and a plait of her hair stuck to her plate.

The newly designed plane is
going to be very plain.

She will have a plum before
using the plumb line.

People are gathering to take
a poll by that pole.

Let's pour some lemonade as we
pore over this material.

When people hunt for animals,
we always pray for the prey.

She expected them to prod
her to test the prodd.

A prophet should be meek and
not seek to make a profit.

She must find her lost pearl and take
her perle before starting to purl.

Our cook is a fast-paced individual and
will make that paste with haste.

They had a packed office when the
pact was prepared for signing.

The letter P is sometimes referred to as
pee but has nothing to do with a pea.

Dorothy told her Pa that her dog hurt his
paw on that adventurous brick road.

Let's pedal to the consignment
store and peddle our bikes.

Ok, make something interesting of these – palette, palate, pallet.

It would be nice if Nakita would purr fourteen times per day.

Her perse purse was very gorgeous.

The attorney lost her petti when speaking about something petty, but to her it was petit.

She asked for a hot cup of pekoe while she performs a picot on the lace.

Pete barked at a pigeon using pidgin, but the bird did not comprehend.

Pie is something we eat, but pi is used in math.

It soon became plainer the man operating the planer was very skilled.

When the miner finds his prase, he should praise God as he prays.

It would probably be a good idea to pack each boot with a pac.

Phew, we thought there were only going to be a few of us for the crew.

Q

When the girl with a queue walks in, that will be our cue.

We will need several quarts of water if we hunt quartz today.

If we are going to dock this craft, we need to head for the quay on the cay.

A well-known ranger thought his horse was a quitter, until he discovered it had quittor.

In medieval times, there was a quintain but it was not related to a quintan fever.

We made a quire for the choir.

R

The rabbit is sitting on that wood with a rabbet.

We must read, then rede the group about that reed, then sign the deed.

This room has an odor of rheum. Isn't English awesome?

Let's paint the room red, then redd it up after we have read the story.

Let's build a regle for the door, so it will be a more regal room.

Our king went riding, but to reign as king, he must use the rein even in the rain.

Let's review the revue.

That row of fish seems to have roe.

Let's roll out the carpet so everyone will know their role.

In Italy, let's roam about until we reach Rome.

It won't be rude to ask if the church has a rood.

It was rough but we made the ruff for his neck.

Roy wrote a rhyme but left it outside, and the paper got covered with rime.

It seemed totally radical to remove the radicle.

There is an enormous root exposed near here and we know the route to it.

Dyson has a real reel now, so he's sure it can pull in a fourteen-ton shark.

Samson will raise the boom then use it to raze the old room.

Reck and wreck are challenging, but you can create something with them.

Our reins became infected when the rains came.

He knew he would rue the day when he consumed soup with roux in it.

After the gale, the large rack was a total wrack.

S

Sherry's office is a sweet suite.

We will see the sea when we reach the apex of the hill.

Savannah, let's sail to the mainland tomorrow for the sale.

We hope no one will steal the steel while we are away.

It's raining today, so let's sew clothes, then sow seeds another day.

Shoot the ducks, toss them down the chute, and prepare them for dinner.

A sack is similar to an animal sac.

He was seen at the scene of the accident.

The scent was so bad, it sent us looking elsewhere for the missing cent.

We could not seel the eyes of the seal to test it.

Sheldon commanded his dog to sic the robber, and now the robber is sick.

Does the seam seem to be ok?

It's not sane to try to seine evil spirits, but we could sain the cross.

If Porky sees the hamburger he will seize and devour it.

It doesn't make sense that we end up with only fourteen cents.

The seer was incorrect about the sere weather and the cere of our parrot.

A serf would not be allowed near the surf.

There has been a surge for serge fabric lately.

While watching our serial, we ate our cereal.

Let's shear the sheep so they will be cooler climbing the sheer mountain.

Calculate the sine, and sign the paper.

Please learn how to sleave the silk, before making the sleeve.

My soul is my sole possession.

Some of us need to get busy and calculate the sum of it.

Our son loves the sun and fun.

We have a stake in this venture, so we need to purchase lean steak.

The stair is awesome, but don't stare at it.

The stollen has been stolen, and we must find it and also locate the stolon.

The strait of water is straight.

While wearing a stupe, he will
stoop to check the stoup.

What style is the stile?

Even the sink and drain are in sync.

Before we search for the streak of gold in
the river we should streek to loosen up.

Please scat, because we will
not play skat with you.

On the pier, we found a skull tied to the scull.

There is a man acting like a sennet in the
senate who needs to be removed with sennit.

Please set the sett on the workbench.

Sue will go over the sault in Quincy's boat,
and sew it up, then sue him if injured.

Sure, we can shirr up the cloth.

It would be wise to say "shoo"
to a shoe with a bad odor.

A famous goose sighs sadly when she
measures the size of her waist.

Please slow down and have a
look at the sloe over there.

If we had enough lore, we could soar,
but only if it would not make us sore.

Our sow was making a sough type noise
as she ran through the bushes.

Please steer to the area where we
will find that stere of cordwood.

Please find the room with the picture of
the seal on the wall, and ceil the ceiling.

Caution, we do not want to slay a
wolf while racing in our sleigh.

T

Tyler read a tale about a dragon
with a one hundred foot tail.

May the two of us go to town too?

We can teem with the team
to accomplish the task.

Let's have tea before we tee off.

The tapir has legs that taper.

Mary was taught not to pull the
rope too taut on her lamb.

There was a tear in her eye when
she climbed to the fourth tier.

There is a mouse in their house
that they're painting.

Let's tear out the tare and
prepare for planting.

It was difficult to throw off the throe he had.

It's time to remove the thyme
and plant the vine.

While observing the tick under microscope,
it became apparent it had a tic.

While preparing to tow our
boat, my toe was broken.

A whole troop of people came to
see the troupe perform.

You threw the ball through the window.

Could there be a tun large enough
to hold a ton of turtles?

He dealt a trey and put it on the empty tray.

After the tutee is prepared, he will
become a member of the tutti group.

The ballerina is good, but it's too too
bad she isn't wearing her tutu. Ugh.

The villain dropped a torte on our friend's
head and the act became a tort.

Tammy noticed the tern making a turn.

We went to the beach once and caught
a tope that was taupe in color.

Here's one to review – the and thee.

Now, check out timbal and timbale.

We towed our boat to the lake
and saw a toed toad.

We approached the toll bridge and
observed a large shiny tole in the road.

Tack has many descriptions
but tach has only one.

The knight was very tacit until
he donned his tasset.

Many years ago, the first talkie evolved
and later perhaps became a talky talkie.

She went to see a seer who had
a tarot but not a taro.

If a teal were flying in Europe,
it might land in a teil.

We decided to tease the plumber
by hiding his tees.

The tenor had a tenner in his wallet.

The tensor had been tenser.

In the Bible, you may find terce and
the scripture might be terse.

A termer could be a termor.

We had a ternary situation in our shop with
a turnery, drill press, and milling machine.

While checking the terrain, the ape
man found it to be mostly terrane.

Wow, in chemistry and biology
check out thallous and thallus.

Ok, here's a totally rad one
– theirs and there's.

Theocracy and theocrasy are definitely akin.

Review the adverbs therefor and therefore.

We could thurm the wood, then ponder therm.

The king was thrown from his throne.

Create something exciting with til & till.

When the tide went out, he tied up his boat.

In chemistry, there is titer,
but what about tighter?

We received a tip about typp in textiles.

A tocsin warned us about a fourteen
foot snake with venomous toxin.

In Las Vegas, a woman wearing a
toque gave a toke to an employee.

If there is a tung tree, why isn't
there a tongue tree?

It required a tool to fabricate a tulle.

In the toon world, Dooby Scoo
may want to sing a tune.

Elaborate on tor, torr, and tore.

There is trochee and in
pharmaceuticals troche.

We put our trust in the trussed herald.

She had a serious tussle with a tussal tussis.

U

This bill is undue, so let's undo it.

Ugli is delicious but might be considered ugly.

While on Uranus, the spaceship crew became concerned about the adjectives uranous and urinous.

V

He is vain about the vein he bruised while inspecting the vane.

She believes if she dons her veil in the vale, it will vail to a lower depth.

Valerie will vary the routine, so the task will be very simple.

A vial of sulfuric acid was spilled on the viol and marred the finish.

If we were versed in Russian language, we would be familiar with a verst.

A person having a problem with vice may not know how to utilize a vise.

Vealer is not related to the word velar.

A person on Venus might be venous.

Go ahead, make your teacher's day — Find out about vesical and vesicle.

It probably would not be healthy to have a viscous viscus.

W

A whole brigade of ants are
entering the hole in the pole.

Please wring out the clothes, then
ring the bell for dinner.

From his boat, he wrote a note about
the daily rote he experienced.

Fasting may cause your waist to waste away.

You will get weak as the week ends,
if on a fishing worm diet.

We will waive the penalty if you help us
escape that approaching tidal wave.

If we place a piece of hardware on his
body, then he would wear the ware.

Whee, we must remove that
wee tree before planting.

While in Britain, she will check out wey,
but no way will she weigh herself.

A famous sow eats what she wants,
and her weight problem can wait.

Let's dine and not whine if the fine
wine doesn't get served on time.

His wheel has a lump on it like the wheal
from a fourteen-pound mosquito.

A whale might wail if it gets a wale on its back.

She does not have a whit of
wit. Isn't English cool?

Please wait for a while until the wile begins.

Please enter the marsh and tie up
some reeds with a withe.

Whoa, the situation does not
require that amount of woe.

It would be good if you would pile
the wood by the old hood.

We will wrest the hammer from
the rest of the tools.

The farmer had a wry expression in
his eye when he checked the rye.

Why was the train backing into the wye?

Let's wrap the box and be careful not to rap it.

After brewing up some wort at the fort,
could it cause us to get a wart?

Let's not wield our authority too much or
we may lose a section of the weald.

We're all familiar with a wiener,
but what is a weaner?

We're going down to the river
to investigate the weir.

We've got to weave our way
to our friend's abode.

If you whet your knife, it will stay cooler if you wet it.

Back in the Dark Ages, someone might ask, "Which witch will we burn at the stake?"

We were going to whir over there. Isn't English totally radical?

I wish we could whish over there immediately.

The church is wholly composed of holy artifacts and statues.

Let's whirl about quickly and proceed to the area where the whorl is.

Who's going to find out whose auto it is?

There is a white wight hanging out over there.

While preparing our party we should be on guard for a wile.

That bad wurst was the worst we ever had.

We hope the hosts will not wreak punishment on us because we reek like dead fish.

The homeless person was an unfortunate wretch and appeared about to retch.

The wright was right when he said we should fight to write a new rite about the site.

The farmer wrung the chicken's neck on the rung of the ladder.

It sure feels good that we won one.

Y

Lew, have you seen our ewe out by the yew?

We need a yoke to hold one yolk to another.

You're going there, aren't you, to check out how your paintings are doing?

Y'all get on that yawl and go seek Neptune or another denizen of the deep.

The dog will not yap at the yapp binder.

Your friends cannot understand days of yore when that magic dragon roamed.

You'll always enjoy the Yule times.

About the Author

The author is a retired aerospace manufacturing engineer and design engineer, concluding his career on the Delta Four Rocket Program. However, he was always fascinated with the complicated English language. Approximately three years ago, during a family feast, his mind generated "I'm going to pare a pair of pears." That was the genesis for "WHAT WORD WHEN."

www.ingramcontent.com/pod-product-compliance
Ingram Content Group UK Ltd.
Pitfield, Milton Keynes, MK11 3LW, UK
UKHW040019200726
13854UKWH00001B/275